THE CRYPTO PLAYBOOK: WINNING STRATEGIES FOR 2025 AND BEYOND

Genevieve Velzian

Copyright © 2024 Genevieve Velzian

All rights reserved

All recommendations are based on the author's opinion and in no way replace the need to seek your own legal advice. Please seek legal counsel before implementing new strategies or investing. The author accepts no liability for actions taken as a result of reading this book.

No part of this book may be reproduced, or stored in a retrieval system, or transmitted in any form or by any means, electronic, mechanical, photocopying, recording, or otherwise, without express written permission of the publisher.

CONTENTS

Copyright 3
Introduction 3
Understanding Blockchain Technology 3
Getting Started with Crypto Investments 3
Market Analysis and Trends 3
Investment Strategies for 2025 3
Decentralized Finance (DeFi) 3
Non-Fungible Tokens (NFTs) 3
Dipping Your Foot in the Water 3
Security and Risk Management 3
Regulatory Landscape 3
Tax Implications of Crypto Investments 3
Advanced Trading Techniques 3
Case Studies of Successful Investors 3
Future of Cryptocurrency 3
Ethical Investing 3
Building Your Personal Crypto Strategy 3
Retire and Crypto 3
Resources and Further Reading 3
The End 3
About The Author 3
Title Page 1

INTRODUCTION

Welcome to "The Crypto Playbook: Winning Strategies for 2024." Whether you are a seasoned investor or a curious newcomer, this book is designed to equip you with the knowledge and tools necessary to navigate the dynamic world of cryptocurrency. As we stand on the cusp of a new era in digital finance, understanding and leveraging the power of cryptocurrencies can unlock unprecedented opportunities for wealth creation and financial freedom.

The Evolution of Cryptocurrency

Cryptocurrencies have come a long way since the inception of Bitcoin in 2009. What began as an experimental digital currency has blossomed into a trillion-dollar market, reshaping the financial landscape and challenging traditional economic systems.

The evolution of cryptocurrencies has been marked by rapid innovation, widespread adoption, and a growing recognition of their potential to transform various industries.

Why Crypto Matters in 2024

As we step into 2024, the importance of cryptocurrencies in the global economy cannot be overstated. Governments, financial institutions, and corporations are increasingly embracing blockchain technology, the backbone of cryptocurrencies, for its security, transparency, and efficiency.

Decentralized finance (DeFi) platforms are revolutionizing the way we interact with financial services, while non-fungible tokens (NFTs) are creating new paradigms in art, entertainment, and beyond.

For investors, the crypto market offers a unique blend of high-risk, high-reward opportunities. Unlike traditional financial markets, the crypto market operates 24/7, providing continuous opportunities for trading and investment. However, with these opportunities come significant risks, necessitating a well-informed and strategic approach to investing.

Overview of Major Cryptocurrencies

Bitcoin may be the most well-known cryptocurrency, but it is far from the only one worth your attention. Ethereum, with its smart contract capabilities, has opened the door to a multitude of decentralized applications.

Altcoins like Binance Coin, Solana, and Cardano offer unique features and potential growth opportunities. Stablecoins provide a less volatile entry point for those cautious about market fluctuations. Understanding the nuances of these and other cryptocurrencies is crucial for developing a robust investment strategy.

The Goal of This Book

The primary goal of this book is to provide you with a comprehensive guide to winning strategies in the crypto market for 2024 and beyond.

We will delve into the fundamentals of blockchain technology, explore various investment strategies, and examine the latest trends and developments in the crypto space. From setting up your digital wallet to advanced trading techniques, this playbook covers all aspects of cryptocurrency investment.

We will also address the practical considerations of investing in crypto, such as security measures, regulatory compliance, and tax implications. Through case studies and expert interviews, you will gain insights from successful crypto investors and learn how to avoid common pitfalls.

Preparing for the Future

The world of cryptocurrency is fast-paced and ever-evolving. Staying ahead of the curve requires continuous learning and adaptation. This book is not just a guide but a starting point for your journey into the world of crypto investments. By the end of this book, you will be equipped with the knowledge and confidence to make informed investment decisions and capitalize on the opportunities that the crypto market presents.

Welcome to "The Crypto Playbook: Winning Strategies for 2024." Let's embark on this exciting journey together and unlock the potential of the digital future.

UNDERSTANDING BLOCKCHAIN TECHNOLOGY

In the rapidly evolving landscape of cryptocurrency, blockchain technology stands as the foundational innovation driving the entire ecosystem. To navigate and succeed in the world of crypto, a thorough understanding of blockchain is essential.

This chapter will delve into the intricacies of blockchain technology, its role in supporting cryptocurrencies, and the latest advancements that are shaping the future.

The Basics of Blockchain

At its core, a blockchain is a decentralized, digital ledger that records transactions across multiple computers in a way that ensures security and transparency. The key features of blockchain include:

Decentralization: Unlike traditional databases that are controlled by a single entity, a blockchain is maintained by a distributed network of nodes. Each node has a copy of the entire blockchain, ensuring that no single point of failure can compromise the system.

Immutability: Once a transaction is recorded on the blockchain, it cannot be altered or deleted. This immutability is achieved through cryptographic hashing, which links each block of transactions to the previous one, creating a secure and unchangeable chain.

Transparency: All transactions on a public blockchain are visible to anyone with access to the network. This transparency fosters trust and accountability, as participants can independently verify the authenticity of transactions.

How Blockchain Supports Cryptocurrency

Blockchain technology underpins cryptocurrencies by providing a secure and transparent way to record and verify transactions. Here's how it works in practice:

Transaction Initiation: A user initiates a transaction by creating a digital signature using their private key. This signature ensures that the transaction is authentic and authorized by the user.

Broadcasting to the Network: The transaction is broadcasted to the network of nodes, which validate it against a set of predefined rules (consensus mechanism).

Validation and Consensus: Nodes in the network validate the transaction and reach a consensus on its legitimacy. Different blockchains use various consensus mechanisms, such as Proof of Work (PoW) or Proof of Stake (PoS), to achieve this agreement.

Recording the Transaction: Once validated, the transaction is grouped with other transactions into a block. This block is then added to the existing blockchain in a linear, chronological order.

Confirmation: The transaction is confirmed once the block is added to the blockchain. Subsequent blocks further confirm the transaction, enhancing its security and permanence.

Innovations in Blockchain Technology

Since the inception of Bitcoin, blockchain technology has evolved significantly, leading to numerous innovations that enhance its functionality and applicability. Some of the key advancements include:

Smart Contracts: Introduced by Ethereum, smart contracts are self-executing contracts with the terms of the agreement directly written into code. They automatically execute and enforce contractual agreements when predefined conditions are met, enabling a wide range of decentralized applications (dApps).

Layer 2 Solutions: To address scalability issues, Layer 2 solutions like the Lightning Network (for

Bitcoin) and Plasma (for Ethereum) have been developed. These solutions operate on top of the main blockchain, processing transactions off-chain and then settling them on-chain, thereby increasing transaction speed and reducing costs.

Interoperability: Projects like Polkadot and Cosmos aim to create an interconnected ecosystem of blockchains, enabling them to communicate and share data seamlessly. This interoperability fosters collaboration and innovation across different blockchain networks.

Privacy Enhancements: Privacy-focused blockchains and protocols, such as Monero and zk-SNARKs (used in Zcash), offer enhanced privacy features by obfuscating transaction details and user identities. These advancements address concerns about transaction confidentiality in the crypto space.

Blockchain Beyond Cryptocurrency

While cryptocurrencies are the most well-known application of blockchain technology, its potential extends far beyond digital currencies. Blockchain is being explored and implemented in various industries, including:

Supply Chain Management: Blockchain enhances transparency and traceability in supply chains, enabling real-time tracking of goods from origin to destination. This can help combat counterfeiting and ensure the authenticity of products.

Healthcare: Blockchain can secure patient records, streamline administrative processes, and facilitate secure sharing of medical data among healthcare providers, improving patient care and data integrity.

Finance: Beyond cryptocurrencies, blockchain is revolutionizing traditional finance through decentralized finance (DeFi) applications. These platforms offer financial services such as lending, borrowing, and trading without intermediaries, reducing costs and increasing accessibility.

Voting Systems: Blockchain-based voting systems promise to enhance the integrity and transparency of elections by providing a tamper-proof record of votes, ensuring that each vote is counted accurately and securely.

Conclusion

Understanding blockchain technology is crucial for anyone looking to succeed in the world of cryptocurrency. Its decentralized, transparent, and immutable nature forms the backbone of the crypto ecosystem, driving innovation and offering countless opportunities across various sectors.

As we move forward into 2024 and beyond, staying informed about the latest advancements in blockchain technology will be key to leveraging its full potential and achieving success in your crypto investments.

In the next chapter, we will explore how to get started with crypto investments, from setting up your digital wallet to choosing the right exchange and essential tools for trading. This foundational knowledge will prepare you to dive deeper into the strategies and opportunities that the crypto market offers.

GETTING STARTED WITH CRYPTO INVESTMENTS

Embarking on your journey into the world of cryptocurrency investments can be both exciting and overwhelming. This chapter aims to guide you through the essential steps to get started, from setting up your digital wallet to choosing the right exchange and utilizing essential tools for trading. By the end of this chapter, you'll have a solid foundation to begin investing in cryptocurrencies confidently.

Setting Up Your Digital Wallet

A digital wallet is your first step into the crypto world. It stores your cryptocurrencies securely and allows you to send, receive, and manage your assets. There are several types of wallets to consider:

Hot Wallets: These are connected to the internet and are typically more user-friendly. Examples include mobile apps (e.g., Trust Wallet), desktop applications (e.g., Exodus), and web-based wallets (e.g., MetaMask). While convenient, they are more vulnerable to hacking.

Cold Wallets: These are offline wallets, providing a higher level of security. Hardware wallets (e.g., Ledger, Trezor) and paper wallets are common types of cold wallets. They are ideal for storing large amounts of cryptocurrency that you don't need to access frequently.

Custodial vs. Non-Custodial Wallets: Custodial wallets are managed by third parties (e.g., exchanges like Coinbase), meaning the provider holds your private keys. Non-custodial wallets give you full control of your private keys, offering greater security and autonomy.

Steps to Set Up a Wallet:

Choose the Right Wallet: Based on your needs, select a hot or cold wallet. For beginners, a reputable hot wallet with a good balance of security and usability is recommended.

Download and Install: Follow the instructions to download and install the wallet software on your device.

Create a New Wallet: Open the application and follow the prompts to create a new wallet. You will be given a seed phrase – a series of words that serve as a backup for your wallet. Write this down and store it securely; it is crucial for recovering your wallet if needed.

Secure Your Wallet: Set a strong password and enable additional security features such as two-factor authentication (2FA).

Choosing the Right Exchange

A cryptocurrency exchange is where you can buy, sell, and trade cryptocurrencies. Choosing a reliable exchange is critical for a smooth investment experience. Here are some factors to consider:

Security: Look for exchanges with robust security measures, such as cold storage for funds, 2FA, and a strong track record of preventing hacks.

Reputation: Research the exchange's reputation within the crypto community. Check user reviews, online forums, and regulatory compliance.

Fees: Compare the fee structures of different exchanges, including trading fees, withdrawal fees, and deposit fees. Some exchanges offer lower fees but may have fewer features.

Supported Cryptocurrencies: Ensure the exchange supports the cryptocurrencies you are interested in. Some exchanges offer a wide variety of coins, while others may be more limited.

User Interface: A user-friendly interface is important, especially for beginners. Choose an exchange that is easy to navigate and understand.

Popular Exchanges to Consider:

Binance: Known for its wide range of supported cryptocurrencies and advanced trading features.

Coinbase: Popular for its user-friendly interface and strong security measures, ideal for beginners.

Kraken: Offers a good balance of security, fees, and advanced features.

Gemini: Known for regulatory compliance and strong security features.

Steps to Set Up an Exchange Account:

Register: Visit the exchange's website and create an account using your email address.

Verify Your Identity: Complete the KYC (Know Your Customer) process by providing identification documents. This step ensures regulatory compliance and enhances security.

Secure Your Account: Enable 2FA and set up other security measures offered by the exchange.

Deposit Funds: Deposit fiat currency or cryptocurrency into your account to start trading.

Essential Tools for Crypto Trading

To navigate the crypto market effectively, several tools and resources can enhance your trading experience:

Price Tracking Tools: Websites like CoinMarketCap and CoinGecko provide real-time price tracking, market capitalization, trading volume, and other key metrics for thousands of cryptocurrencies.

Portfolio Management Apps: Tools like Blockfolio and Delta help you track your investments, monitor performance, and receive alerts on price changes and news.

Charting and Analysis Platforms: For advanced traders, platforms like TradingView offer comprehensive charting tools, technical analysis indicators, and community-driven insights.

News Aggregators: Staying informed about market news is crucial. Websites like CryptoSlate, CoinDesk, and CoinTelegraph provide up-to-date news, analysis, and trends in the crypto world.

Social Media and Communities: Engage with the crypto community on platforms like Twitter, Reddit (e.g., r/cryptocurrency), and Telegram. These communities offer valuable insights, discussions, and real-time updates.

Conclusion

Setting up your digital wallet, choosing the right exchange, and utilizing essential tools are critical steps in your journey into the world of crypto investments. With these foundational elements in place, you are well-equipped to begin trading and investing in cryptocurrencies confidently.

In the next chapter, we will delve into market analysis and trends, teaching you how to read the crypto market and predict movements to make informed investment decisions. By mastering these basics, you'll be ready to take advantage of the opportunities that the crypto market offers.

MARKET ANALYSIS AND TRENDS

Understanding the crypto market's dynamics is essential for making informed investment decisions. This chapter will explore how to read the crypto market, identify key indicators and metrics, and predict market movements to help you stay ahead in the ever-evolving landscape of cryptocurrency.

Reading the Crypto Market

The crypto market is known for its volatility, and understanding how to read it can be challenging but rewarding. Here are some fundamental aspects to consider:

Market Capitalization: This metric measures the total value of a cryptocurrency. It is calculated by multiplying the current price by the total supply of coins in circulation. High market cap generally indicates a more stable and widely accepted cryptocurrency.

Trading Volume: This refers to the total amount of a cryptocurrency traded within a specific period. High trading volumes often indicate strong market interest and liquidity, making it easier to buy and sell the asset.

Price Movements: Monitoring the price movements of cryptocurrencies can provide insights into market sentiment. Tools like candlestick charts help visualize these movements over different time frames, highlighting trends and potential reversal points.

Supply and Demand: Like any market, crypto prices are influenced by supply and demand dynamics. Factors such as limited supply (e.g., Bitcoin's capped supply) and increasing demand (e.g., institutional adoption) can drive prices higher.

Key Indicators and Metrics

Several key indicators and metrics can help you analyze the crypto market more effectively:

Relative Strength Index (RSI): This momentum oscillator measures the speed and change of price movements. An RSI above 70 indicates overbought conditions, while an RSI below 30 indicates oversold conditions.

Moving Averages (MA): Moving averages smooth out price data to identify trends over a specific period. The 50-day and 200-day moving averages are commonly used to spot long-term trends and potential buy/sell signals.

Bollinger Bands: These bands plot standard deviations above and below a moving average. They help identify overbought or oversold conditions and potential price breakouts.

MACD (Moving Average Convergence Divergence): This trend-following indicator shows the relationship between two moving averages. It helps identify potential buy and sell signals based on the crossing of the MACD line and the signal line.

On-Balance Volume (OBV): This metric uses trading volume to predict price movements. A rising OBV indicates buying pressure, while a falling OBV suggests selling pressure.

Predicting Market Movements in 2025 and Beyond

Predicting market movements is challenging, but certain approaches can enhance your ability to forecast trends:

Technical Analysis: This involves analyzing historical price and volume data to identify patterns and trends. Tools like chart patterns, trend lines, and technical indicators are commonly used.

Fundamental Analysis: This approach assesses the intrinsic value of a cryptocurrency by examining factors such as technology, team, use case, and market potential. Strong fundamentals often lead to long-term growth.

Sentiment Analysis: This involves gauging market sentiment by analyzing news, social media, and community discussions. Positive sentiment can drive prices higher, while negative sentiment can lead to declines.

Macro-Economic Factors: Keep an eye on broader economic trends, regulatory developments, and geopolitical events. These factors can significantly impact the crypto market.

Conclusion

By mastering market analysis and understanding key indicators and metrics, you can make more informed investment decisions and better predict market movements. The crypto market's volatility presents both opportunities and risks, and a solid analytical approach can help you navigate it successfully.

INVESTMENT STRATEGIES FOR 2025

Investing in cryptocurrencies requires a well-thought-out strategy tailored to your financial goals, risk tolerance, and market conditions.

This chapter will explore various investment strategies, including long-term vs. short-term investments, portfolio diversification, and risk management techniques to help you build a robust crypto investment plan.

Long-Term vs. Short-Term Investments

Choosing between long-term and short-term investment strategies depends on your financial objectives and risk appetite:

Long-Term Investments (HODLing): Long-term investors, often referred to as "HODLers," buy and hold cryptocurrencies for an extended period, typically years. This strategy relies on the belief that the value of cryptocurrencies will increase significantly over time. Long-term investing is suitable for those who believe in the future potential of blockchain technology and are willing to withstand market volatility.

Benefits: Reduced trading costs, less stress from short-term market fluctuations, potential for significant gains.
Drawbacks: Exposure to prolonged market downturns, requires patience and strong conviction.

Short-Term Investments (Trading): Short-term investors actively trade cryptocurrencies to capitalize on price fluctuations. This strategy involves frequent buying and selling, often within days, hours, or even minutes. Short-term trading is suitable for those with a higher risk tolerance and the ability to dedicate time to market analysis.

Benefits: Potential for quick profits, ability to leverage market volatility.

Drawbacks: Higher trading costs, increased stress and time commitment, potential for significant losses.

Diversifying Your Crypto Portfolio

Diversification is a key principle in investment that helps spread risk and increase potential returns. In the context of crypto, diversification involves:

Allocating Across Different Cryptocurrencies: Instead of investing all your funds in a single cryptocurrency, spread your investments across multiple coins.

Consider including a mix of large-cap cryptocurrencies (e.g., Bitcoin, Ethereum) and promising altcoins (e.g., Cardano, Polkadot).

Including Different Types of Assets: Diversify your portfolio by including different types of crypto assets, such as utility tokens, security tokens, and stablecoins. This approach can reduce risk and provide exposure to various market segments.

Balancing Between High-Risk and Low-Risk Investments: Include a mix of high-risk, high-reward investments and more stable, lower-risk assets. For example, allocate a portion of your portfolio to established cryptocurrencies while dedicating a smaller portion to newer, more speculative projects.

Risk Management Techniques

Effective risk management is crucial to protect your investments and achieve long-term success in the crypto market. Here are some techniques to consider:

Set Investment Goals: Define your financial goals, risk tolerance, and investment horizon. Having clear objectives will guide your investment decisions and help you stay focused.

Use Stop-Loss Orders: Stop-loss orders automatically sell a cryptocurrency when its price reaches a predetermined level. This technique helps limit losses and protect your capital.

Avoid Emotional Trading: Emotional decisions can lead to impulsive trades and significant losses. Stick to your investment plan and avoid making decisions based on fear or greed.

Stay Informed: Keep up-to-date with market news, regulatory developments, and technological advancements. Staying informed will help you make better investment decisions and adapt to changing market conditions.

Regularly Rebalance Your Portfolio: Periodically review and adjust your portfolio to ensure it aligns with your investment goals and risk tolerance. Rebalancing helps maintain a diversified and balanced portfolio.

Conclusion

Developing a robust investment strategy is essential for success in the crypto market. Whether you prefer long-term investments or short-term trading, diversification and effective risk management are key components of a successful strategy.

By setting clear goals, staying informed, and managing risk, you can navigate the volatile crypto market and work towards achieving your financial objectives.

In the next chapter, we will explore the world of decentralized finance (DeFi), an innovative sector within the crypto space that offers exciting opportunities for investors. Understanding DeFi and its potential can open new avenues for growth and diversification in your investment portfolio.

DECENTRALIZED FINANCE (DEFI)

Decentralized Finance, or DeFi, is one of the most transformative developments in the cryptocurrency space. It represents a new financial ecosystem built on blockchain technology that aims to replicate and improve upon traditional financial services in a decentralized manner.

In this chapter, we will explore the fundamentals of DeFi, the opportunities it presents, and the top DeFi projects to watch in 2024.

Understanding DeFi

DeFi leverages blockchain technology to offer financial services without intermediaries like banks or brokers. It uses smart contracts on decentralized platforms to execute financial transactions, making these services more accessible, transparent, and efficient. Key components of DeFi include:

Decentralized Exchanges (DEXs): Platforms like Uniswap and SushiSwap allow users to trade cryptocurrencies directly with each other without relying on a centralized exchange. These exchanges use automated market makers (AMMs) to facilitate trading.

Lending and Borrowing Platforms: DeFi platforms like Aave and Compound enable users to lend their cryptocurrencies to earn interest or borrow assets by providing collateral. These platforms operate without traditional credit checks, relying instead on over-collateralization to mitigate risk.

Stablecoins: Stablecoins are cryptocurrencies pegged to a stable asset, such as the US dollar. They provide a stable store of value and are used extensively in DeFi applications. Popular stablecoins include Tether (USDT), USD Coin (USDC), and DAI.

Yield Farming and Liquidity Mining: These strategies involve providing liquidity to DeFi protocols in exchange for rewards. Yield farmers earn interest and tokens by locking their assets in liquidity pools.

Insurance Protocols: DeFi insurance platforms like Nexus Mutual offer coverage for risks specific to the crypto space, such as smart contract failures and exchange hacks.

Opportunities in the DeFi Space

DeFi presents numerous opportunities for investors to earn passive income and participate in innovative financial services:

Earning Interest: By lending your assets on DeFi platforms, you can earn attractive interest rates compared to traditional savings accounts. Interest rates vary depending on the demand for the asset and the platform used.

Staking: Staking involves participating in a proof-of-stake (PoS) network by locking up your tokens to support the network's security and operations. In return, stakers receive rewards in the form of additional tokens.

Liquidity Provision: By providing liquidity to DEXs or lending platforms, you can earn a share of the trading fees and additional token rewards. This can be a lucrative strategy but comes with the risk of impermanent loss.

Participating in Governance: Many DeFi projects issue governance tokens that grant holders voting rights on protocol changes and improvements. Holding these tokens allows you to influence the future direction of the project.

Top DeFi Projects to Watch in 2024/ 2025

As the DeFi space continues to evolve, several projects stand out for their innovation and potential:

Uniswap (UNI): A leading decentralized exchange that pioneered the use of AMMs. Uniswap's continuous updates and strong community make it a top project to watch.

Aave (AAVE): A prominent lending and borrowing platform known for its user-friendly interface and diverse range of supported assets. Aave's innovative features, such as flash loans, set it apart from competitors.

Compound (COMP): Another major player in the lending and borrowing sector, Compound's protocol is widely respected for its security and efficiency.

Synthetix (SNX): A platform for creating and trading synthetic assets, which are tokenized representations of real-world assets. Synthetix's unique offering provides exposure to traditional financial instruments within the DeFi space.

Yearn Finance (YFI): A yield optimization protocol that automatically moves users' funds between different DeFi platforms to maximize returns. Yearn Finance's automation and community-driven development make it a key project to follow.

Risks and Challenges in DeFi

While DeFi offers significant opportunities, it also comes with risks and challenges:

Smart Contract Risks: Bugs or vulnerabilities in smart contracts can lead to significant losses. It's essential to use well-audited protocols and stay informed about potential risks.

Regulatory Uncertainty: DeFi operates in a largely unregulated space, and future regulatory changes could impact the industry. Stay informed about regulatory developments and their potential implications.

Market Volatility: The value of assets locked in DeFi protocols can be highly volatile, affecting your returns and collateral value in lending platforms.

Impermanent Loss: Providing liquidity to AMMs can result in impermanent loss if the price of the provided assets changes significantly. Understand the mechanics of impermanent loss before participating.

Conclusion

Decentralized Finance is revolutionizing the financial industry by offering innovative, accessible, and efficient services. By understanding the fundamentals of DeFi and exploring its opportunities, you can participate in this transformative sector and potentially reap significant rewards.

In the next chapter, we will dive into Non-Fungible Tokens (NFTs), another groundbreaking area within the crypto space that is reshaping art, entertainment, and beyond.

NON-FUNGIBLE TOKENS (NFTS)

Non-Fungible Tokens, or NFTs, have taken the digital world by storm, revolutionizing how we think about ownership, art, and collectibles. This chapter will explore the rise of NFTs, their unique characteristics, and the potential they hold for investors and creators alike. We will also examine future trends in the NFT market and how to get started with NFT investments.

The Rise of NFTs

NFTs are unique digital assets that represent ownership of a specific item or piece of content, verified by blockchain technology. Unlike cryptocurrencies such as Bitcoin or Ethereum, which are fungible and can be exchanged on a one-to-one basis, each NFT is unique and cannot be replicated.

This uniqueness has led to the explosion of digital art, collectibles, and other digital assets.

Digital Art and Collectibles: Artists can tokenize their works as NFTs, allowing them to sell digital art with verifiable ownership and provenance. Platforms like OpenSea, Rarible, and Foundation have become popular marketplaces for buying and selling digital art and collectibles.

Gaming and Virtual Worlds: NFTs are increasingly used in the gaming industry to represent in-game assets, characters, and virtual real estate. Games like Axie Infinity and Decentraland have demonstrated the potential of NFTs to create vibrant digital economies.

Music and Media: Musicians and content creators are leveraging NFTs to sell exclusive content, concert tickets, and other digital media directly to their fans. This direct-to-fan model offers new revenue streams and greater control over their work.

Investing in Digital Art and Collectibles

Investing in NFTs requires a different approach compared to traditional cryptocurrencies. Here are some steps to get started:

Research and Identify Opportunities: Understand the different types of NFTs and their respective markets. Follow trends, artists, and projects to identify potential investment opportunities.

Choose a Marketplace: Select a reputable NFT marketplace that supports the type of NFTs you are interested in. Popular platforms include OpenSea, Rarible, SuperRare, and Foundation.

Set Up a Digital Wallet: To buy and sell NFTs, you'll need a digital wallet that supports NFTs and the specific blockchain the NFTs are built on (e.g., Ethereum, Binance Smart Chain).

Purchase and Store NFTs: Use your digital wallet to purchase NFTs from the marketplace. Ensure you store your NFTs securely, considering hardware wallets for high-value assets.

Monitor the Market: Keep an eye on market trends, artist developments, and new projects. The NFT market can be highly volatile, so staying informed is crucial for making strategic investment decisions.

Future Trends in the NFT Market

The NFT market is still in its early stages, and several trends are shaping its future:

Interoperability: As the NFT ecosystem grows, interoperability between different blockchains and platforms will become increasingly important. Projects like Polkadot and Cosmos are working towards creating interconnected networks that can facilitate seamless transfer and use of NFTs across different platforms.

Enhanced Utility: NFTs are evolving beyond digital art and collectibles. They are being integrated into

DeFi protocols, used as collateral for loans, and even providing access to exclusive content and communities. This enhanced utility will drive broader adoption and new use cases.

Environmental Concerns: The environmental impact of blockchain technology, particularly proof-of-work blockchains like Ethereum, has raised concerns. Efforts are underway to transition to more eco-friendly solutions, such as Ethereum's shift to proof-of-stake with ETH 2.0 and the rise of eco-friendly blockchains like Tezos and Flow.

Regulation and Compliance: As NFTs gain popularity, regulatory scrutiny is likely to increase. Understanding and navigating the regulatory landscape will be crucial for both creators and investors.

Conclusion

Non-Fungible Tokens represent a significant innovation in digital ownership and the creator economy. By understanding the unique characteristics of NFTs and staying informed about market trends, you can tap into the potential of this burgeoning market.

As the NFT space continues to evolve, new opportunities for investment and creativity will emerge, offering exciting possibilities for those willing to explore this digital frontier.

DIPPING YOUR FOOT IN THE WATER

Entering the world of cryptocurrency doesn't require a large capital outlay. You can start with a modest investment and gradually build your portfolio as you gain experience and confidence.

This chapter will guide you through the steps to get started with low investments, focusing on practical strategies, tools, and resources that can help you dip your toes into the crypto market.

Understanding the Basics

Before you begin investing, it's essential to understand the fundamental concepts of cryptocurrency:

What is Cryptocurrency?: Digital or virtual currencies that use cryptography for security and operate on decentralized networks based on blockchain technology.

Popular Cryptocurrencies: Bitcoin (BTC), Ethereum (ETH), and various altcoins like Cardano (ADA), Solana (SOL), and Polkadot (DOT).

Setting Up Your Digital Wallet

A digital wallet is necessary to store and manage your cryptocurrencies. Here's how to set one up:

Choose a Wallet: For beginners, a mobile or web-based wallet is convenient. Popular options include Trust Wallet, Coinbase Wallet, and MetaMask.

Download and Install: Follow the instructions to download and install the wallet on your device.

Create a New Wallet: Set up your wallet by creating a new account and securing your seed phrase (a series of words used to recover your wallet if you lose access).

Secure Your Wallet: Enable two-factor authentication (2FA) and set a strong password.

Choosing an Exchange

To buy, sell, and trade cryptocurrencies, you'll need to use an exchange. Consider the following steps:

Select an Exchange: Choose a reputable exchange that allows low minimum deposits. Some user-friendly options include Binance, Coinbase, and Kraken.

Register and Verify: Create an account and complete the verification process (KYC) by providing necessary identification documents.

Deposit Funds: Deposit a small amount of money to start, typically $10 to $50, which is sufficient to begin trading with low investments.

Starting Small: Practical Steps

Here's how you can start investing in crypto with a low budget:

Buy Fractional Shares: Cryptocurrencies are divisible, meaning you can buy fractions of a coin. For example, you can purchase a fraction of a Bitcoin or Ethereum based on your budget.

Focus on Low-Cost Coins: Explore low-cost cryptocurrencies with potential for growth. Research and invest in promising altcoins that fit within your budget.

Use Dollar-Cost Averaging (DCA): Invest a small, fixed amount regularly (e.g., weekly or monthly). DCA reduces the impact of market volatility and helps build your portfolio gradually.

Participate in Airdrops and Giveaways: Some projects distribute free tokens through airdrops and giveaways. Follow reputable projects and participate to earn free crypto.

Leveraging Free Resources

There are numerous free resources available to help you learn and grow your crypto investments:

Educational Websites and Courses: Websites like Coursera, Khan Academy, and CryptoZombies offer free courses on blockchain and cryptocurrency.

YouTube Channels: Follow educational YouTube channels like Andreas M. Antonopoulos, Coin Bureau, and BitBoy Crypto for insights and tutorials.

Crypto News Websites: Stay updated with the latest news and trends on sites like CoinDesk, CoinTelegraph, and CryptoSlate.

Community Forums and Social Media: Engage with the crypto community on Reddit (e.g., r/cryptocurrency), Twitter, and Telegram for advice, tips, and support.

Managing Risks

Even with small investments, it's important to manage risks effectively:

Do Your Research: Conduct thorough research before investing in any cryptocurrency. Understand the project's purpose, technology, team, and market potential.

Diversify: Spread your investments across multiple cryptocurrencies to reduce risk. Avoid putting all your funds into a single coin.

Set Limits: Determine your risk tolerance and set limits for each investment. Decide in advance how much you're willing to invest and stick to it.

Secure Your Assets: Ensure the security of your digital wallet and exchange accounts by enabling 2FA, using strong passwords, and regularly updating your software.

Tracking and Growing Your Portfolio

Monitor your investments and adjust your strategy as you gain experience:

Portfolio Tracking Apps: Use apps like Blockfolio, Delta, or CoinStats to track your portfolio's performance and stay informed about market trends.

Reinvest Profits: As you earn returns from your investments, consider reinvesting a portion to grow your portfolio over time.

Learn from Experience: Reflect on your investment decisions and learn from both successes and mistakes. Continuously improve your strategy based on your experiences.

Conclusion

Starting with low investments in cryptocurrency is a practical and accessible way to enter the market and build your knowledge and confidence. By setting up a secure wallet, choosing a reputable exchange, leveraging free resources, and managing risks effectively, you can gradually grow your portfolio and explore the exciting opportunities the crypto world has to offer.

With patience, discipline, and continuous learning, you can make the most of your small investments and position yourself for long-term success in the cryptocurrency market.

SECURITY AND RISK MANAGEMENT

As the world of cryptocurrency continues to expand, ensuring the security of your investments becomes increasingly critical. This chapter will guide you through the essential measures to protect your assets, avoid scams and fraud, and implement best practices for crypto security. Understanding and mitigating risks is paramount to maintaining the integrity of your investments.

Protecting Your Investments

To safeguard your cryptocurrency investments, it's important to take proactive measures:

Use Secure Wallets: Choose reputable wallets with strong security features. For long-term storage, hardware wallets (cold wallets) like Ledger and Trezor offer enhanced security by keeping your private keys offline.

Enable Two-Factor Authentication (2FA): Always enable 2FA on your exchange accounts and wallets.

This adds an extra layer of security by requiring a second form of verification, typically through a mobile app like Google Authenticator.

Keep Your Private Keys Safe: Your private keys are crucial to accessing your cryptocurrency. Never share them with anyone and store them securely, preferably offline. Consider writing them down and keeping them in a safe place.

Regularly Update Software: Ensure that your wallet software, exchange apps, and devices are up-to-date with the latest security patches. Regular updates protect against vulnerabilities and exploits.

Use Strong Passwords: Create strong, unique passwords for your crypto accounts and change them periodically. Avoid using the same password across multiple platforms.

Avoiding Scams and Frauds

The crypto space, while full of opportunities, is also rife with scams and fraudulent schemes. Being vigilant and informed can help you avoid falling victim to these threats:

Phishing Scams: Be cautious of emails, messages, or websites that attempt to trick you into revealing your private keys or passwords. Always verify the authenticity of communication and access websites directly rather than through links.

Ponzi Schemes: Avoid schemes that promise guaranteed high returns with little risk. These are often too good to be true and are designed to defraud investors.

Fake ICOs and Tokens: Research thoroughly before investing in Initial Coin Offerings (ICOs) or new tokens. Check the project's whitepaper, team credentials, and community feedback to ensure legitimacy.

Social Engineering: Be wary of unsolicited advice or requests from strangers online, even if they seem knowledgeable. Scammers often use social engineering tactics to gain trust and access to your assets.

Best Practices for Crypto Security

Implementing best practices can further enhance the security of your crypto investments:

Segregate Your Funds: Keep your long-term holdings in a cold wallet and use a hot wallet for daily transactions. This reduces the risk of losing all your assets in case of a security breach.

Backup Your Wallet: Regularly backup your wallet and store multiple copies in different secure locations. This ensures you can recover your assets if your device is lost or damaged.

Monitor Account Activity: Regularly check your exchange and wallet accounts for any suspicious activity. Set up alerts to notify you of any unusual transactions.

Educate Yourself Continuously: Stay informed about the latest security threats and best practices in the crypto space. Participate in community discussions, follow reputable news sources, and consider taking online courses on crypto security.

Conclusion

Protecting your cryptocurrency investments requires vigilance, knowledge, and the implementation of robust security measures. By following the guidelines outlined in this chapter, you can significantly reduce the risk of losing your assets to scams, fraud, or technical failures.

In the next chapter, we will explore the regulatory landscape of cryptocurrencies, helping you navigate the legal challenges and understand the implications of regulations on your investments.

REGULATORY LANDSCAPE

As cryptocurrencies continue to gain traction, governments and regulatory bodies worldwide are increasingly focusing on how to regulate this emerging asset class. Understanding the regulatory environment is crucial for navigating the crypto market legally and effectively. This chapter will provide an overview of current regulations, how to navigate legal challenges, and the future of crypto regulation.

Understanding Crypto Regulations

Cryptocurrency regulations vary significantly across different jurisdictions. While some countries embrace crypto, others impose strict regulations or outright bans. Key regulatory areas include:

Anti-Money Laundering (AML) and Know Your Customer (KYC): To prevent illicit activities, many countries require exchanges and financial institutions to implement AML and KYC protocols. These measures involve verifying the identity of users and monitoring transactions for suspicious activity.

Securities Regulations: In some jurisdictions, certain cryptocurrencies and tokens may be classified as securities. This classification subjects them to specific regulatory requirements, including registration and disclosure obligations.

Taxation: Cryptocurrencies are subject to various tax regulations depending on the country. Tax authorities may treat them as property, currency, or financial instruments, affecting how gains and losses are reported and taxed.

Consumer Protection: Regulatory bodies aim to protect consumers from fraud and misrepresentation in the crypto market. This includes regulations around advertising, disclosures, and ensuring fair practices by exchanges and service providers.

Navigating Legal Challenges

To operate within the legal framework, it's essential to stay informed about the regulatory environment and take proactive steps to ensure compliance:

Stay Informed: Regularly update yourself on the regulatory developments in your country and any jurisdictions where you operate or invest. Follow news from regulatory bodies, legal experts, and industry associations.

Choose Compliant Platforms: Use exchanges and service providers that comply with local regulations.

Reputable platforms typically have robust AML and KYC measures and are transparent about their compliance practices.

Keep Accurate Records: Maintain detailed records of your crypto transactions, including dates, amounts, and the purpose of transactions. Accurate records are essential for tax reporting and compliance audits.

Consult Legal and Tax Experts: Engage with legal and tax professionals who specialize in cryptocurrency. They can provide tailored advice and help you navigate complex regulatory requirements.

The Future of Crypto Regulation

The regulatory landscape for cryptocurrencies is continually evolving. Several trends are shaping the future of crypto regulation:

Increased Regulatory Clarity: As the crypto market matures, regulators are working towards providing clearer guidelines and frameworks. This increased clarity can foster greater adoption and innovation by reducing uncertainty for investors and businesses.

Global Cooperation: Regulatory bodies are increasingly collaborating to create harmonized regulations across borders. This cooperation aims to address the global nature of crypto and combat illicit activities more effectively.

Focus on Stablecoins and DeFi: Regulators are paying particular attention to stablecoins and decentralized finance (DeFi) platforms. Ensuring these innovations operate within a legal framework is critical to maintaining financial stability and consumer protection.

Environmental Considerations: The environmental impact of cryptocurrencies, particularly those using proof-of-work (PoW) consensus mechanisms, is becoming a regulatory focus. Future regulations may promote or mandate more sustainable practices within the industry.

Conclusion

Navigating the regulatory landscape is a crucial aspect of participating in the cryptocurrency market. By staying informed and compliant, you can mitigate legal risks and position yourself for long-term success.

In the next chapter, we will explore the tax implications of crypto investments, providing strategies for minimizing tax liability and ensuring compliance with reporting requirements.

TAX IMPLICATIONS OF CRYPTO INVESTMENTS

Navigating the tax implications of cryptocurrency investments can be complex, but it is essential for ensuring compliance and optimizing your financial outcomes. This chapter will guide you through understanding tax laws and reporting requirements, strategies for minimizing tax liability, and best practices for keeping accurate records.

Tax Laws and Reporting Requirements

Cryptocurrency taxation varies by country, but generally, crypto transactions are taxable events. Key areas to consider include:

Capital Gains Tax: Most jurisdictions treat cryptocurrencies as property, meaning any profit from selling, trading, or using crypto is subject to capital gains tax. The rate may vary depending on how long you've held the asset (short-term vs. long-term gains).

Income Tax: Earning cryptocurrency through mining, staking, airdrops, or as payment for goods and services is typically considered income and subject to income tax. The value of the crypto at the time of receipt is used to determine the taxable amount.

Transaction Reporting: You must report all taxable transactions on your tax return, including sales, trades, and conversions of one cryptocurrency to another. Detailed records of each transaction, including dates, amounts, and values in your local currency, are necessary.

Losses and Deductions: Capital losses from crypto investments can often be used to offset capital gains, potentially reducing your overall tax liability. Some jurisdictions also allow you to carry forward losses to future tax years.

Strategies for Minimizing Tax Liability

Effective tax planning can help reduce your tax burden and maximize your after-tax returns. Consider the following strategies:

Tax-Loss Harvesting: This strategy involves selling cryptocurrencies that have decreased in value to realize a loss, which can offset gains from other investments. You can repurchase the same or similar assets after a specific period, depending on local tax rules.

Long-Term Holding: Holding assets for more than one year can qualify you for long-term capital gains tax rates, which are typically lower than short-term rates. This strategy not only reduces your tax rate but also aligns with a long-term investment approach.

Gifting and Donations: In some jurisdictions, gifting cryptocurrencies can reduce your taxable estate. Additionally, donating crypto to a registered charity may provide a tax deduction based on the asset's fair market value at the time of the donation.

Using Tax-Advantaged Accounts: If available in your jurisdiction, consider using tax-advantaged accounts for your crypto investments. For example, certain retirement accounts may offer tax deferral or exemption on investment gains.

Stay Informed and Seek Professional Advice: Tax laws and regulations are continually evolving, especially for cryptocurrencies. Stay updated on the latest developments and consider consulting with a tax professional who specializes in crypto taxation.

Keeping Accurate Records

Maintaining detailed and accurate records is crucial for complying with tax laws and optimizing your tax strategies:

Track Every Transaction: Record the date, amount, and value of each transaction in your local currency. Include details such as the type of transaction (buy, sell, trade, etc.), the assets involved, and any associated fees.

Use Crypto Tax Software: Consider using dedicated crypto tax software to simplify the process of tracking transactions and calculating gains and losses. These tools can integrate with exchanges and wallets to automatically import transaction data.

Regularly Review and Reconcile: Periodically review your records to ensure accuracy and completeness. Reconciling your records with exchange statements and wallet balances can help identify any discrepancies.

Store Documentation Securely: Keep all related documentation, such as exchange statements, wallet addresses, and transaction confirmations, in a secure and organized manner. This will facilitate easy access during tax season or in the event of an audit.

Conclusion

Understanding and managing the tax implications of your crypto investments is essential for compliance and optimizing your financial outcomes.

By implementing effective tax strategies and maintaining accurate records, you can minimize your tax liability and ensure a smooth tax filing process.

ADVANCED TRADING TECHNIQUES

For those looking to take their crypto investments to the next level, advanced trading techniques offer a way to maximize returns and manage risks more effectively. This chapter will cover technical analysis, algorithmic trading, and leveraging and margin trading, providing you with the tools and knowledge to enhance your trading strategy.

Technical Analysis for Crypto

Technical analysis involves using historical price data and trading volume to predict future price movements. Here are some key concepts and tools:

Chart Patterns: Recognizing patterns such as head and shoulders, triangles, and flags can provide insights into potential price movements. These patterns are formed by the price action over time and can indicate continuation or reversal of trends.

Support and Resistance Levels: Support levels are price points where an asset tends to find buying interest, preventing further decline. Resistance levels are where selling pressure prevents the price from rising. Identifying these levels helps traders make informed entry and exit decisions.

Candlestick Analysis: Candlestick charts display the high, low, open, and close prices for a specific period, providing visual cues about market sentiment. Common candlestick patterns, such as dojis, hammers, and engulfing patterns, can signal potential market reversals.

Technical Indicators: Indicators like Moving Averages (MA), Relative Strength Index (RSI), Bollinger Bands, and Moving Average Convergence Divergence (MACD) provide additional insights into price trends and market momentum. Combining multiple indicators can enhance the accuracy of your predictions.

Using Algorithms and Bots

Algorithmic trading involves using automated systems to execute trades based on predefined criteria. This approach can help eliminate emotional decision-making and increase trading efficiency:

Trading Bots: Bots can execute trades based on specific strategies, such as arbitrage, market making, or trend following. Platforms like 3Commas,

CryptoHopper, and Shrimpy offer customizable trading bots for various strategies.

Developing Algorithms: If you have programming skills, you can develop your own trading algorithms using languages like Python or JavaScript. These algorithms can analyze market data, identify trading opportunities, and execute trades automatically.

Backtesting and Optimization: Before deploying an algorithm, it's crucial to backtest it using historical data to evaluate its performance. Optimization involves tweaking the algorithm's parameters to enhance its effectiveness under different market conditions.

Leveraging and Margin Trading

Leverage and margin trading allow traders to amplify their exposure to the market using borrowed funds. While these techniques can increase potential profits, they also come with higher risks:

Understanding Leverage: Leverage involves borrowing funds to increase your trading position beyond your initial capital. For example, using 10x leverage means you can control a position worth ten times your investment. While this can magnify gains, it also magnifies losses.

Margin Trading: In margin trading, traders borrow funds from a broker or exchange to trade larger positions. Margin accounts require maintaining a minimum balance (margin) and are subject to margin calls if the account value falls below a certain threshold.

Risk Management: Due to the high risk associated with leverage and margin trading, it's essential to implement strict risk management practices. This includes setting stop-loss orders, using appropriate leverage levels, and never risking more than you can afford to lose.

Choosing the Right Platform: Not all exchanges offer leverage and margin trading, and those that do may have different requirements and features. Popular platforms for leverage trading include Binance, BitMEX, and Kraken. Ensure you understand the platform's terms and conditions before engaging in leveraged trading.

Conclusion

Advanced trading techniques can significantly enhance your ability to profit from the crypto market, but they also require a deep understanding of the risks involved.

By mastering technical analysis, leveraging algorithmic trading, and carefully managing the risks of leverage and margin trading, you can take your trading strategy to the next level.

In the next chapter, we will explore case studies of successful investors, providing insights and lessons from their experiences in the crypto market.

CASE STUDIES OF SUCCESSFUL INVESTORS

Learning from the experiences of successful investors can provide valuable insights and practical lessons for your own crypto investment journey. This chapter presents case studies of individuals who have achieved significant success in the crypto market, highlighting their strategies, challenges, and key takeaways.

Case Study 1: The Bitcoin Early Adopter

Background: John Smith, a software developer, first heard about Bitcoin in 2010. Intrigued by the technology, he decided to invest a small amount of money, purchasing 1,000 BTC at around $0.10 each.

Strategy: John's strategy was simple: buy and hold. He believed in the long-term potential of Bitcoin and was prepared to weather the market's volatility.

Challenges: The early years were marked by significant price swings, and there were moments of doubt, especially during major market crashes. John had to remain patient and avoid the temptation to sell during downturns.

Outcome: By late 2017, Bitcoin's price had surged to nearly $20,000. John's investment grew exponentially, and he decided to sell a portion of his holdings to secure financial stability while keeping the rest invested for future growth.

Key Takeaways:

Belief in the underlying technology can help maintain a long-term perspective.

Patience and resilience are crucial in a highly volatile market.

Diversifying and securing profits at strategic points can mitigate risk.

Case Study 2: The Altcoin Trader

Background: Sarah Lee, a finance graduate, entered the crypto market in 2017. She started with a modest investment in Bitcoin but soon became interested in altcoins for their higher growth potential.

Strategy: Sarah diversified her portfolio across several promising altcoins, such as Ethereum, Cardano, and Chainlink. She used technical analysis to identify entry and exit points and actively traded to capitalize on market trends.

Challenges: The altcoin market is notoriously volatile, and Sarah faced several instances where her investments plummeted rapidly. She had to adapt her strategies, continually learning and improving her trading techniques.

Outcome: Despite the challenges, Sarah's diversified approach and active trading led to substantial profits. By 2020, her portfolio had grown significantly, allowing her to reinvest in new projects and further diversify her holdings.

Key Takeaways:

Diversification can spread risk and increase exposure to high-growth opportunities.

Active trading requires continuous learning and adaptation to market conditions.

Technical analysis can enhance decision-making and improve trading outcomes.

Case Study 3: The DeFi Pioneer

Background: Michael Nguyen, an entrepreneur, discovered decentralized finance (DeFi) in 2019. Fascinated by its potential to disrupt traditional finance, he started investing in DeFi projects early.

Strategy: Michael focused on staking and yield farming in DeFi platforms like Aave, Compound, and Yearn Finance. He also invested in governance tokens, participating actively in protocol development and decision-making.

Challenges: The DeFi space is complex and rapidly evolving, with significant risks, including smart contract vulnerabilities and regulatory uncertainty. Michael had to stay informed and manage these risks carefully.

Outcome: Michael's early investments in DeFi projects paid off handsomely as the sector grew. His active involvement in governance also provided additional rewards and insights into emerging opportunities.

Key Takeaways:

Early adoption of emerging technologies can lead to significant rewards.

Active participation in project governance can provide valuable benefits and insights.

Understanding and managing risks is crucial in complex and evolving sectors like DeFi.

Conclusion

These case studies highlight diverse strategies and approaches to successful crypto investing. Whether through long-term holding, active trading, or early adoption of new technologies, each investor demonstrated key principles such as patience, continuous learning, and risk management.

By applying these lessons to your own investment strategy, you can enhance your chances of success in the crypto market.

In the next chapter, we will explore the future of cryptocurrency, examining emerging technologies and trends that are likely to shape the next decade of digital finance.

FUTURE OF CRYPTOCURRENCY

As we look towards the future, the cryptocurrency landscape continues to evolve rapidly. This chapter explores emerging technologies and trends that are poised to shape the next decade of digital finance, providing insights into how you can prepare and capitalize on these developments.

Predictions for the Next Decade

Several key trends and developments are expected to influence the future of cryptocurrency:

Mass Adoption: Cryptocurrencies are likely to see increased adoption across various sectors, including retail, finance, and technology. As more businesses and consumers embrace digital currencies, the market is set to expand significantly.

Integration with Traditional Finance: The lines between traditional finance and cryptocurrency are blurring. Financial institutions are increasingly integrating blockchain technology and offering crypto-related services, such as custody solutions, trading platforms, and investment products.

Central Bank Digital Currencies (CBDCs): Governments worldwide are exploring the creation of CBDCs, which are digital versions of their national currencies. CBDCs aim to combine the benefits of digital currencies with the stability of traditional fiat money, potentially revolutionizing the global financial system.

Enhanced Scalability: Technological advancements will address current scalability issues, enabling faster and more efficient transactions. Solutions like Ethereum 2.0, Layer 2 protocols, and new consensus mechanisms will play a crucial role in this evolution.

Emerging Technologies and Their Impact

Several emerging technologies are set to drive innovation and growth in the crypto space:

Interoperability Solutions: Projects like Polkadot, Cosmos, and Chainlink are working towards creating an interconnected ecosystem of blockchains. Interoperability will enable seamless communication and value transfer between different networks, enhancing the overall utility and efficiency of blockchain technology.

Decentralized Identity (DID): DID systems aim to give individuals control over their digital identities without relying on centralized authorities. This technology can improve privacy, security, and accessibility across various online services.

Quantum Computing: As quantum computing advances, it poses both challenges and opportunities for blockchain technology. While quantum computers could potentially break current cryptographic algorithms, they also offer the potential for more secure and efficient blockchain systems through quantum-resistant algorithms.

Artificial Intelligence (AI): AI can enhance blockchain technology by optimizing processes, improving security, and enabling more sophisticated data analysis. AI-driven predictive models and trading algorithms can also provide new opportunities for investors.

Preparing for the Future

To position yourself for success in the evolving crypto landscape, consider the following strategies:

Stay Informed: Continuously educate yourself about emerging technologies, market trends, and regulatory developments. Follow reputable news sources, join online communities, and participate in industry events.

Diversify Your Portfolio: Diversify your investments across different cryptocurrencies, sectors, and technologies. This approach can help spread risk and increase exposure to high-growth opportunities.

Invest in Education and Skills: Developing a deep understanding of blockchain technology and related fields can provide a competitive edge. Consider taking courses, obtaining certifications, and gaining hands-on experience through projects and collaborations.

Monitor Regulatory Changes: Stay aware of regulatory developments in your jurisdiction and globally. Understanding the regulatory landscape will help you navigate potential challenges and capitalize on new opportunities.

Conclusion

The future of cryptocurrency is filled with promise and potential. By staying informed, embracing new technologies, and adopting a forward-thinking approach, you can position yourself to thrive in the next decade of digital finance.

The cryptocurrency market will continue to evolve, and those who are prepared to adapt and innovate will be best positioned to reap the rewards.

ETHICAL INVESTING

As the cryptocurrency market grows, the importance of ethical investing becomes increasingly significant. Ethical investing involves considering the environmental, social, and governance (ESG) impacts of your investment choices.

This chapter will explore how to invest ethically in the crypto space, covering key principles, practical strategies, and the benefits of adopting an ethical approach.

Understanding Ethical Investing

Ethical investing, also known as socially responsible investing (SRI) or impact investing, focuses on generating both financial returns and positive social or environmental impacts. In the context of cryptocurrency, this involves:

Environmental Responsibility: Considering the environmental impact of blockchain networks, particularly those with high energy consumption.

Social Impact: Investing in projects that promote social good, such as financial inclusion, privacy, and security.

Governance: Supporting transparent, fair, and accountable projects and organizations.

Principles of Ethical Crypto Investing

To invest ethically in the crypto market, consider the following principles:

Sustainability: Choose cryptocurrencies and blockchain projects that prioritize sustainability. Look for those that use energy-efficient consensus mechanisms, such as Proof of Stake (PoS) or other low-energy alternatives to Proof of Work (PoW).

Transparency and Accountability: Support projects that are transparent about their operations, governance structures, and financial practices. Transparency fosters trust and accountability in the crypto ecosystem.

Social Impact: Invest in projects that aim to solve real-world problems and create positive social impact. Examples include projects focused on financial inclusion, data privacy, and secure digital identities.

Community and Governance: Favor projects with strong, active communities and fair governance models. Decentralized Autonomous Organizations

(DAOs) and community-driven initiatives often embody these principles.

Practical Strategies for Ethical Investing

Implementing ethical investing principles requires a thoughtful and informed approach:

Research and Due Diligence: Conduct thorough research on potential investments. Evaluate the project's whitepaper, team credentials, use case, and community feedback. Assess the project's ESG impact and alignment with your values.

Support Sustainable Projects: Prioritize investments in projects that use sustainable technologies. For example, Ethereum's transition to ETH 2.0 and Proof of Stake (PoS) aims to reduce energy consumption significantly.

Engage with Communities: Join and participate in the communities of projects you invest in. Engaging with the community allows you to stay informed, contribute to governance decisions, and support ethical practices.

Diversify with Impact: Diversify your portfolio by including a mix of projects that address different social and environmental issues. This approach not only spreads risk but also amplifies your positive impact.

Vote with Your Tokens: If you hold governance tokens, actively participate in voting on proposals and decisions that shape the project's future. Use your voting power to support ethical practices and initiatives.

Benefits of Ethical Crypto Investing

Adopting an ethical approach to crypto investing offers several benefits:

Positive Impact: Ethical investing allows you to contribute to projects that align with your values and create positive social and environmental change.

Long-Term Value: Projects that prioritize sustainability, transparency, and social impact are more likely to build long-term value and resilience, benefiting both the community and investors.

Enhanced Reputation: By supporting ethical projects, you can build a reputation as a responsible investor, attracting like-minded collaborators and opportunities.

Regulatory Alignment: Ethical investing can help you stay ahead of regulatory changes, as governments increasingly focus on sustainability and social responsibility in the crypto space.

Conclusion

Investing ethically in the cryptocurrency market involves aligning your investment choices with your values and considering the broader impact of your actions. By prioritizing sustainability, transparency, and social impact, you can contribute to a more responsible and equitable crypto ecosystem.

Ethical investing not only supports positive change but also enhances the long-term viability and success of the projects you invest in.

BUILDING YOUR PERSONAL CRYPTO STRATEGY

Creating a successful personal crypto strategy involves setting clear financial goals, developing a winning mindset, and crafting a tailored investment plan. This chapter will guide you through these essential steps to help you build a robust and effective strategy for navigating the cryptocurrency market.

Setting Financial Goals

Establishing clear financial goals is the foundation of any successful investment strategy. Consider the following steps:

Define Your Objectives: Identify what you want to achieve with your crypto investments. Are you looking to build long-term wealth, generate passive income, or speculate on short-term price movements? Your objectives will shape your strategy and risk tolerance.

Set Specific, Measurable Goals: Break down your objectives into specific, measurable goals. For example, aim to achieve a certain percentage return on investment within a specified timeframe or accumulate a specific amount of a particular cryptocurrency.

Determine Your Time Horizon: Consider your investment timeline. Are you investing for short-term gains, medium-term growth, or long-term wealth accumulation? Your time horizon will influence your asset allocation and investment approach.

Assess Your Risk Tolerance: Evaluate your risk tolerance based on your financial situation, investment experience, and comfort level with market volatility. This assessment will help you choose appropriate assets and strategies.

Developing a Winning Mindset

A winning mindset is crucial for navigating the ups and downs of the crypto market. Focus on the following aspects:

Patience and Discipline: Successful investing requires patience and discipline. Avoid making impulsive decisions based on short-term market fluctuations. Stick to your strategy and stay focused on your long-term goals.

Continuous Learning: The crypto market is constantly evolving. Commit to continuous learning by staying informed about market trends, new technologies, and regulatory developments. This knowledge will help you make better-informed decisions.

Emotional Resilience: The volatile nature of the crypto market can evoke strong emotions. Develop emotional resilience by maintaining a balanced perspective and avoiding knee-jerk reactions to market movements.

Adaptability: Be prepared to adapt your strategy as market conditions change. Flexibility and openness to new opportunities are essential for long-term success in the dynamic crypto landscape.

Creating a Personalized Crypto Playbook

A personalized crypto playbook is a detailed plan that outlines your investment strategy, risk management approach, and action steps. Consider including the following elements:

Asset Allocation: Decide how to allocate your capital across different cryptocurrencies, sectors, and investment types. Diversification can help spread risk and increase potential returns.

Entry and Exit Strategies: Define your criteria for entering and exiting positions. This may include technical analysis indicators, fundamental analysis insights, or specific price targets.

Risk Management: Implement risk management techniques to protect your capital. Set stop-loss orders, use appropriate leverage levels, and avoid overexposure to any single asset.

Monitoring and Review: Regularly monitor your portfolio's performance and review your strategy. Make adjustments as needed based on changing market conditions and your evolving financial goals.

Documentation and Record-Keeping: Maintain detailed records of your transactions, investment decisions, and performance metrics. This documentation will help you track your progress and refine your strategy over time.

Conclusion

Building a personal crypto strategy involves setting clear financial goals, developing a winning mindset, and creating a tailored playbook.

By following these steps, you can navigate the crypto market with confidence and work towards achieving your financial objectives.

RETIRE AND CRYPTO

Transitioning from a traditional career to focusing on cryptocurrency investments full time can be an exciting and rewarding endeavor. This bonus chapter will guide you through the steps necessary to retire and dedicate yourself to crypto, covering financial planning, lifestyle adjustments, and strategies for maintaining long-term success.

Financial Planning for Retirement

Before making the leap to full-time crypto investing, it's crucial to ensure you have a solid financial foundation:

Assess Your Financial Situation: Calculate your total assets, liabilities, and monthly expenses. Understanding your current financial standing will help you determine how much you need to sustain your lifestyle without a traditional job.

Create a Retirement Budget: Develop a detailed budget that accounts for all your living expenses, including housing, utilities, food, healthcare, insurance, and discretionary spending. Factor in potential increases in expenses due to inflation and changes in your lifestyle.

Build an Emergency Fund: Set aside a substantial emergency fund to cover at least 6-12 months of living expenses. This fund will provide a financial cushion in case of unexpected events or market downturns.

Plan for Taxes: Consider the tax implications of your crypto investments. Different jurisdictions have varying tax laws regarding capital gains, income, and crypto transactions. Consult a tax professional to ensure compliance and optimize your tax strategy.

Diversify Your Investments: While focusing on crypto, it's wise to diversify your portfolio to include other asset classes such as stocks, bonds, real estate, and precious metals. Diversification helps spread risk and provides additional income streams.

Transitioning to Full-Time Crypto

Making the transition from a traditional job to full-time crypto investing requires careful planning and adjustment:

Set Clear Goals: Define your objectives for transitioning to full-time crypto. Are you seeking financial freedom, personal fulfillment, or the opportunity to delve deeper into the crypto space? Clear goals will guide your decisions and actions.

Develop a Routine: Establish a daily routine that balances research, trading, portfolio management, and leisure activities. A structured routine helps maintain productivity and prevents burnout.

Continuously Educate Yourself: The crypto market is dynamic and ever-evolving. Dedicate time to continuous learning by reading books, taking online courses, attending webinars, and participating in industry conferences.

Engage with the Community: Join crypto communities on platforms like Reddit, Telegram, Discord, and Twitter. Engaging with other investors and enthusiasts provides valuable insights, networking opportunities, and support.

Manage Your Mental Health: The volatility of the crypto market can be stressful. Practice mindfulness, exercise regularly, and take breaks to maintain your mental and emotional well-being.

Strategies for Long-Term Success

Sustaining long-term success in the crypto market requires a combination of strategic planning and disciplined execution:

Develop a Robust Investment Strategy: Create a comprehensive investment strategy that includes asset allocation, risk management, and diversification.

Stick to your strategy and avoid making impulsive decisions based on short-term market movements.

Monitor and Adjust Your Portfolio: Regularly review your portfolio's performance and make adjustments as needed. Rebalance your portfolio to maintain your desired asset allocation and take advantage of new opportunities.

Stay Informed About Market Trends: Keep up with the latest news, trends, and developments in the crypto space. Follow reputable sources, participate in discussions, and stay alert to changes that could impact your investments.

Secure Your Assets: Prioritize the security of your crypto assets by using secure wallets, enabling two-factor authentication (2FA), and practicing good cybersecurity hygiene. Regularly review and update your security measures.

Explore Passive Income Opportunities: Consider generating passive income through staking, yield farming, lending, and other DeFi activities. Passive income can provide a steady revenue stream and reduce reliance on market fluctuations.

Embracing the Lifestyle

Retiring and focusing on crypto full time offers the opportunity to embrace a new lifestyle that aligns with your passions and interests:

Pursue Personal Projects: With more time and financial freedom, you can pursue personal projects and interests related to crypto. This might include developing your own blockchain project, creating educational content, or contributing to open-source initiatives.

Travel and Network: Take advantage of the flexibility to travel and attend crypto conferences, meetups, and events worldwide. Networking with other enthusiasts and professionals can expand your horizons and open up new opportunities.

Give Back to the Community: Consider giving back to the crypto community through mentorship, education, or philanthropy. Sharing your knowledge and resources can help foster a more inclusive and supportive ecosystem.

Conclusion

Retiring and dedicating yourself to crypto full time is a bold and exciting decision that requires careful planning and disciplined execution. By establishing a solid financial foundation, transitioning thoughtfully, and embracing a new lifestyle, you can achieve long-term success and fulfillment in the crypto space.

This journey offers the opportunity to pursue your passions, stay at the forefront of technological innovation, and potentially achieve financial independence.

RESOURCES AND FURTHER READING

Staying informed and continuously learning is essential for success in the rapidly evolving world of cryptocurrency. This chapter provides a list of valuable resources and further reading to help you deepen your knowledge, stay updated on market trends, and connect with the crypto community.

Recommended Books and Articles

Books:

"The Bitcoin Standard: The Decentralized Alternative to Central Banking" by Saifedean Ammous: This book provides a comprehensive history of money and explains why Bitcoin is a revolutionary technology.

"Mastering Bitcoin: Unlocking Digital Cryptocurrencies" by Andreas M. Antonopoulos: A technical guide to understanding Bitcoin and how it works, ideal for both beginners and experienced developers.

"Cryptoassets: The Innovative Investor's Guide to Bitcoin and Beyond" by Chris Burniske and Jack Tatar: This book offers a detailed analysis of different crypto assets and investment strategies.

"Blockchain Basics: A Non-Technical Introduction in 25 Steps" by Daniel Drescher: A beginner-friendly guide to understanding blockchain technology and its applications.

Articles:

CoinDesk Research Reports: In-depth research and analysis on various aspects of the cryptocurrency market.
CoinTelegraph's Guides: Comprehensive guides on a wide range of topics, from blockchain technology to market analysis.

Medium Blogs by Industry Experts: Follow blogs written by crypto industry leaders and experts on Medium for insights and opinions.

Online Courses and Tutorials

Coursera's "Bitcoin and Cryptocurrency Technologies": A Princeton University course that covers the basics of Bitcoin and cryptocurrency technologies.

edX's "Blockchain for Business": Offered by the Linux Foundation, this course explores blockchain technology and its business applications.

Udemy's "Cryptocurrency Investment Course 2023: Fund Your Retirement!": A practical course focused on investment strategies and portfolio management.

YouTube Channels: Channels like Ivan on Tech, Boxmining, and CryptoZombie offer tutorials, news updates, and analysis.

Communities and Forums

Reddit (r/cryptocurrency, r/Bitcoin, r/ethereum): Join discussions, ask questions, and share insights with the crypto community.

Bitcointalk: One of the oldest and largest cryptocurrency forums, where you can find discussions on a wide range of topics.

Telegram Groups: Many crypto projects and communities have active Telegram groups where you can engage with other enthusiasts and developers.

Discord Servers: Similar to Telegram, Discord servers offer a platform for real-time discussions and community building.

News and Information Websites

CoinDesk: A leading news website covering the latest developments in the cryptocurrency world.

CoinTelegraph: Provides news, analysis, and market updates on cryptocurrencies and blockchain technology.

CryptoSlate: Offers news, data, and insights on the crypto market.

Decrypt: Focuses on delivering in-depth news and analysis on the crypto space.

Podcasts and YouTube Channels

Podcasts:

"The Pomp Podcast" by Anthony Pompliano: Interviews with industry leaders and insights into the world of crypto and finance.

"Unchained" by Laura Shin: Deep dives into the people building the decentralized internet and the details of the technology.

"CryptoTopical": Discussions on current events and trends in the cryptocurrency market.

YouTube Channels:

Andreas M. Antonopoulos: Educational videos on Bitcoin, blockchain technology, and security.

DataDash: Market analysis and investment insights from Nicholas Merten.

Altcoin Daily: Daily news and updates on various altcoins and market trends.

Conclusion

The world of cryptocurrency is vast and ever-changing. By leveraging the resources and further reading provided in this chapter, you can stay informed, continue learning, and remain connected with the crypto community.

This ongoing education will help you adapt to new developments and make informed decisions in your investment journey.

Congratulations on reaching the end of "The Crypto Playbook: Winning Strategies for 2024." Armed with the knowledge and strategies outlined in this book, you are well-prepared to navigate the exciting world of cryptocurrency and work towards achieving your financial goals.

THE END

Please leave a review :)

ABOUT THE AUTHOR

Genevieve Velzian

Genevieve Velzian is a full-time digital nomad, who has visited over 40 countries and counting (her next stop is China!) She has various income streams that enable this lifestyle, as well as a YouTube channel and a range of content pieces. As crypto grows over the next few years, and with AI as a hidden support system, she is excited to help others out and all grow together.

www.ingramcontent.com/pod-product-compliance
Lightning Source LLC
Chambersburg PA
CBHW030441220526
45464CB00006B/2374